PRAYERSCRIPTS
Speaking God's Word Back To You

THE PRAYER OF JABEZ

KEEP ME FROM EVIL

30 Days of Prayers For

STANDING UNTOUCHABLE IN SPIRITUAL WARFARE

CYRIL OPOKU

Keep Me From Evil: Standing Untouchable in Spiritual Warfare

© 2025 Cyril Opoku. *PrayerScripts*. All rights reserved.

Published by *Quest Publications*

ISBN: 978-1-988439-84-6

Cover design by *Quest Publications (questpublications@outlook.com)*

Unless otherwise indicated, all Scripture quotations are taken from the World English Bible WEB, which is in the public domain. For more information, visit: www.worldenglish.bible

This book is a work of devotional encouragement. It is not intended to replace biblical study, pastoral counsel, or professional therapy.

Printed in the United States of America.

First Edition: August 2025

For more books like this, visit *PrayerScripts: https://prayerscripts.org*

CONTENTS

PREFACE

"Bring us not into temptation, but deliver us from the evil one."
— Luke 11:4 WEB

From the earliest moments of my spiritual journey, I have been confronted with the reality that the enemy does not rest. I have witnessed firsthand how quickly fear, confusion, and hidden attacks can disrupt a life, a family, or a calling. Yet I have also discovered the profound power of calling upon God intentionally, strategically, and with unwavering faith. This book was born out of those personal encounters—out of prayers I prayed in the quiet of my heart, seeking divine protection and guidance for myself, my loved ones, and all who would join me in asking God to stand guard over their lives.

Keep Me From Evil is my attempt to share that intimate experience of spiritual vigilance. These prayers are not just words on a page; they are declarations shaped by Scripture, refined in Spirit-led encounters, and tested through seasons of challenge. I wrote them with one aim: to help you position yourself in God's protective hand, to claim purity, and to dismantle the schemes of the enemy over your life. Each prayer reflects a facet of my own walk—a step toward standing untouchable in a world that constantly seeks to unsettle the peace of God's people.

As you work through this book, you will find it both a spiritual guide and a companion. It is organized to lead you from a place of shelter into armor, then into purity, and finally into bold declarations that enforce God's promises. Every week is built around principles I have lived, prayed, and seen fulfilled in my own life. My prayer is that these words will not only be a tool but also a testimony—a conduit through which God's power moves freely to protect and prosper you.

Through these pages, I want to pass on a personal truth I've learned: prayer that aligns with God's Word and is spoken with faith has the power to dismantle darkness. It is my hope that this journey will deepen your awareness of His hand, sharpen your spiritual sensitivity, and equip you to live untouchable in every area of your life.

Kept By the Power of God,
Cyril O. *(Illinois, August 2025)*

How to Use This Book

This book is designed as a daily companion to guide you into a prophetic lifestyle of prayer. This is not just a devotional; it is a prayer journey meant to position you to walk in the fullness of God's promises. Here's how to make the most of it:

1. Dedicate a Daily Time:

Set aside a consistent time each day to engage with the prayer for that day. Treat this as sacred time with God, where distractions are minimized, and your heart is fully focused on communion with Him. Ten to twenty minutes daily is sufficient to meditate on the Scripture, pray, and receive revelation.

2. Begin with Scripture Reflection:

Each day begins with a carefully selected Scripture. Read it slowly, meditate on its meaning, and let the Holy Spirit illuminate how it applies to your life. Allow the Word to penetrate your spirit and prepare you to pray from a place of faith and expectancy.

3. Pray the Guided Prayer:

Use the prayer provided as a framework, allowing it to resonate with your own words and personal circumstances. Speak each declaration with authority and confidence, fully believing that God is enlarging your borders, breaking limitations, and establishing your territory. You may also pause to personalize the prayer for your specific family, career, or ministry needs.

- **Make It Personal**

  These prayers are written in the first person so you can make them your own. Speak them aloud, inserting the names of your family members, your workplace, your church, or your city where applicable. The more you personalize the prayer, the more you will sense its power shaping your reality.

- **Pray with Authority**

  These are not timid requests; they are bold decrees. Lift your voice as a covenant child of God, covered by the blood of Jesus and backed by heaven's authority. When you pray, do so with confidence that Christ has already won the victory on your behalf.

- **Leave Room for the Holy Spirit**

  These written prayers are a guide, not a limit. As you pray, pause to listen. The Holy Spirit may give you prophetic words, insights, or specific instructions. Follow His lead. Allow Him to expand the prayer, add declarations, or guide you into deeper intercession.

4. Journal Your Insights:

Keep a notebook or journal to record any thoughts, revelations, or confirmations you receive during prayer. Writing down what God speaks to you helps solidify understanding and creates a record of breakthrough and growth over time.

5. Repeat as Needed:

Some prayers or themes may need to be revisited multiple times. Answer to prayer is progressive; the more you engage with these prayers in faith, the greater the manifestation in your life and household. You can return to this book at any season to reinforce your victory and dominion.

6. Live in Expectancy:

Prayer is only one part of walking in enlargement—your actions, faith, and obedience amplify the power of these prayers. Move boldly into opportunities, embrace the doors God opens, and live with a confident expectation that God is answering your prayer beyond what you can see or imagine.

By following this guide daily, you will cultivate a lifestyle of prayer and kingdom impact. Let this book be your companion as you step into the new dimensions God has destined for you.

INTRODUCTION

> "Jabez called on the God of Israel, saying, 'Oh that you
> would bless me indeed, and enlarge my border! Let your
> hand be with me, and keep me from evil, that I may not
> cause pain!' God granted him that which he requested."
> —1 Chronicles 4:10 WEB

Every believer is called to a life of victory, yet many live under the shadow of fear, oppression, and constant attacks from the enemy. From the very beginning, Jesus taught us to pray, *"Deliver us from the evil one"* (Matthew 6:13). That prayer is not a suggestion—it is a necessity. Evil is real. The adversary prowls about like a roaring lion, seeking whom he may devour. But the good news is this: through the power of God's Word and the covering of Christ's blood, you can stand untouchable, preserved, and victorious no matter what schemes are formed against you.

The prayer of Jabez is more than a cry for blessing—it is a divine key for protection and purity. Jabez dared to ask God not only for enlargement and favor, but also for the shield of holiness: *"Keep me from evil, that I may not cause pain."* His prayer is a pattern for us today. In these last days, when darkness multiplies and the hearts of many grow cold, God is raising up a people who will not merely survive but will thrive under His covering. He is calling you to a life where evil cannot corrupt you, enemies cannot overtake you, and sin cannot enslave you.

This book is designed as a 30-day journey into fortified prayer, teaching you to wield the promises of God like a warrior's sword.

Each day you will pray Scripture in a prophetic, Spirit-led way—prayers that not only defend but advance, not only shield but conquer. You will declare over yourself and your family that you are guarded by God's hand, hidden under His wings, and empowered by His Spirit. You will stand in your rightful position as one seated with Christ in heavenly places, far above principalities and powers.

The journey unfolds in four powerful weeks:

Week 1 — Shelter & Sanctuary: You will discover the foundations of God's protection. Like a child hidden in the cleft of the rock, you will learn to rest under the shadow of the Almighty. No arrow by day, no terror by night, no evil decree can penetrate the shelter of God's presence.

Week 2 — Armor & Authority: You will be clothed in spiritual armor and reminded that you walk in Christ's authority. Prayer is not timid pleading; it is bold enforcement of heaven's decrees. When you stand in the armor of light, the fiery darts of the enemy are extinguished, and your voice carries the authority of the King.

Week 3 — Resist & Stand Pure: Victory over evil requires more than defense; it demands purity of heart and mind. This week calls you to resist the devil and stand pure before God. You will pray for strength to reject temptation, uproot hidden snares, and walk undefiled in a corrupt world.

Week 4 — Promises & Warfare Declarations: God's Word is your weapon, and His promises are your guarantee. This final week equips you to make bold declarations of triumph, reminding the enemy that his defeat is sealed. You will wield the sword of the Spirit to break strongholds, silence lies, and enforce Christ's finished work over every area of your life.

This book is a battle manual. It is your daily call to rise as a warrior of light, clothed in the fire of God's presence, walking in divine immunity. As you pray through these pages, expect transformation. Expect deliverance. Expect the breaking of chains and the lifting of burdens. Expect to be untouchable—not by your own strength, but because the Almighty God has set His seal upon you.

Now take up your place in the army of the Lord. Let every prayer in this book be a weapon in your hand and a shield around your life. Step into the victory that Christ already purchased for you. And as you lift your voice like Jabez, heaven will answer, and God will keep you from evil.

In Jesus' name, Amen.

WEEK 1:
SHELTER & SANCTUARY

Theme: Foundations of God's Protection.

When life's storms rage and the enemy launches arrows of fear, intimidation, and destruction, the safest place is not found in man-made defenses but in the secret place of the Most High. God Himself promises to be our Refuge and our Fortress, a Shelter where no evil can penetrate. His presence is our Sanctuary, and His hand is the shield that guards us day and night.

This week calls you to settle your confidence in the protective covering of the Almighty. Like a child who runs into a parent's embrace, you will learn to run into God's arms—not as a last resort but as your first dwelling place. The Word reminds us that "the name of the Lord is a strong tower; the righteous run into it and are safe." Here, prayer becomes not only your cry for help but your declaration of confidence that you are hidden under His wings.

As you pray through these Scriptures, you will prophetically declare that no weapon of evil shall find its target against your life or your family. You will proclaim divine immunity against sickness, fear, curses, and destructive plots. In this Sanctuary, God not only keeps you safe but restores your peace, renews your strength, and assures you that you are untouchable in Him.

DAY 1

DWELLING IN DIVINE REFUGE

Because you have made Yahweh your refuge, and the Most High your dwelling place, no evil shall happen to you, neither shall any plague come near your dwelling.
— Psalms 91:9-10 WEB

O Lord Most High, my everlasting refuge, I lift my voice today in the confidence of Your unshakable promise. You are my dwelling place, my strong tower, my shield, and my fortress. Because I have chosen to hide my life in You, I boldly declare that evil cannot trespass into my home, and destruction cannot penetrate my walls.

I decree that the snares of the wicked are rendered powerless, and every plague that lurks in shadows is stopped at the threshold of my dwelling. No affliction shall find rest in my household, for the blood of Jesus marks every corner of my life with divine exemption.

Father, by Your mighty hand, frustrate every demonic scheme designed against me, my children, and my family. Let their devices recoil back upon them. Let every whisper of witchcraft, every assignment of sickness, and every cycle of tragedy be consumed by the fire of Your presence.

I speak forth protection over the work of my hands, the path of my feet, and the people I love. Angels of the Lord, encamp round about us, and let no spirit of death, destruction, or evil be able to pierce through. My home is a sanctuary of holiness, covered under the canopy of the Almighty.

I will not fear sudden terror, for my habitation is secured in Christ Jesus. No demon, no principality, no darkness can override the decree of heaven concerning me. I abide under the wings of the Most High, forever untouchable.

In Jesus' name, Amen.

DAY 2

PRESERVED FROM ALL HARM

Yahweh will keep you from all evil. He will keep your soul.
— Psalms 121:7 WEB

O Keeper of Israel, who never slumbers nor sleeps, I exalt Your holy name today. You are my Watchman, my Defender, and my Guardian. You surround me with Your covenant of peace, keeping me far from every arrow of wickedness.

Lord, You have promised to keep me from all evil. Therefore, I decree that no weapon formed against me shall prevail. Every evil decree is nullified, every satanic projection is shattered, and every demonic curse is reversed. You preserve not just my body but my very soul — my mind, will, and emotions are sealed in Christ.

Let the fire of Your Spirit surround me like a wall of protection. Keep my going out and my coming in from this day forward and forevermore. Let the traps of the enemy dissolve into dust before they can ensnare me. Let the plans of darkness be turned into confusion, scattering seven ways before me.

Father, preserve my family from sudden death, calamity, and terror by night. Keep our minds anchored in Your Word so that fear has no foothold. Preserve my heart from the corruption of sin, from the pollution of temptation, and from the voices of compromise.

Lord, You are the Shepherd and Keeper of my soul. I declare that my life, my children, my family, and my generations are hidden in

Christ, preserved in holiness, and guarded by heaven's armies. Evil cannot snatch me out of Your hand.

In Jesus' name, Amen.

DAY 3

MY REFUGE AND STRENGTH

God is our refuge and strength, a very present help in trouble.
— Psalm 46:1 WEB

Mighty Deliverer, my Rock of Ages, I run to You today as my sure refuge and strength. You are my very present help, not distant, not delayed, but always near. I exalt You as the One who shields me from every storm and fortifies me against every assault of the wicked.

I declare that no trouble shall overwhelm me, for my help is immediate and divine. Where men fail, You arise. Where evil advances, You intercept with power. My enemies may gather, but their schemes dissolve in Your presence. My heart is steady, for You are my impenetrable defense.

O Lord, let every stronghold of wickedness erected against me collapse by the weight of Your glory. Let the forces of darkness tremble and scatter as You draw near to defend me. Let every evil covenant, curse, and enchantment melt away under the fire of Your Spirit.

Father, strengthen my inner man so that fear finds no room. Clothe me in courage, gird me with boldness, and cause my faith to be immovable. In the day of trouble, let Your voice thunder against the adversary, silencing the accuser and breaking the arm of the oppressor.

I am not helpless, for I am hidden in the refuge of Christ. My strength is not my own; it flows from the eternal well of the Almighty. Therefore, I am unshaken, unbroken, and untouchable in Your care.

In Jesus' name, Amen.

DAY 4

No Fear of Evil

Even though I walk through the valley of the shadow of
death, I will fear no evil, for you are with me. Your rod and
your staff, they comfort me.
— Psalm 23:4 WEB

Great Shepherd of my soul, I worship You today, for Your presence
is my assurance and my peace. Even in the darkest valley, even in
places where death and destruction lurk, I will not be moved by
fear, because You are with me.

Father, I decree that fear has no dominion over me. I refuse to bow
to the intimidation of the enemy. Though the valley may surround
me, the shadow may threaten me, yet it cannot harm me, for the
Light of Your presence breaks through every darkness.

Your rod defends me against every demonic predator. Your staff
keeps me aligned on the path of righteousness, far from deception,
compromise, and corruption. I am guarded on every side by Your
faithful love. Let the powers of evil see and tremble, for I am not
alone; the Almighty walks with me.

Lord, cover my family and me in the valley seasons. Let Your rod
strike down every wolf of destruction, every lion of devouring,
every serpent of deception. Let the shadow of death flee before the
brilliance of Christ's resurrection power in me.

I fear no evil, for Your Spirit comforts and steadies me. I walk boldly in safety, knowing that every step is ordered and every breath preserved by You. Truly, I am untouchable in Your hands.

In Jesus' name, Amen.

DAY 5

THE STRONG TOWER

The name of Yahweh is a strong tower: the righteous run
to him, and are safe.
— Proverbs 18:10 WEB

O Lord of Hosts, Your name is power, a shield, and a fortress. I run
into the greatness of who You are today, and I am safe. Your name
is not just a sound, but a covenant of protection, a banner over my
life, a tower that no enemy can scale.

I declare that the mighty name of Jesus silences every adversary. At
that name, demons flee, curses break, and chains fall. I exalt the
name that is above every name as the covering over my household,
the defense over my children, and the seal upon my future.

Lord, let every wicked plot be swallowed up by the power of Your
name. Let the weapons of the enemy disintegrate at the mention of
Jesus. Surround me with angelic hosts as a wall of fire, making me
and my family untouchable to arrows by day and terrors by night.

Father, I decree that the name of the Lord is lifted high over my
finances, my health, my relationships, and my destiny. No intruder
can penetrate the fortress of Your name. I stand on holy ground,
guarded and preserved in safety.

I will continually run to You, O Lord. I will hide in the tower of Your
strength and exalt Your name forever, for You alone make me
untouchable. In Jesus' name, Amen.

DAY 6

THE LORD WILL FIGHT

Yahweh will fight for you, and you shall be still.
— Exodus 14:14 WEB

Mighty Warrior, Captain of the Armies of Heaven, I worship You. You are the God who goes before me, the Lord who fights my battles. Today, I rest in the assurance that the war is not mine but Yours.

I declare that every enemy pursuing me falls by the sword of the Lord. Every Pharaoh that refuses to let go is drowned in the sea of Your judgment. Every evil pursuer, every generational bondage, every spiritual oppressor is cut off by Your hand of might.

Lord, silence the accuser who stands against me. Break the arrows of witchcraft, dismantle the snares of sorcery, and scatter the gathering of darkness. Let every altar raised against my family catch fire from heaven. Let the battle turn against my adversaries until they are utterly destroyed.

Father, as You fought for Israel, fight for me today. Let my enemies know that the Lord of Hosts is my defender. I decree that I will not fight in my own strength, nor will I struggle in vain. You are my victory, my banner, and my shield.

I will stand still and see the salvation of the Lord. I rest in confidence, for You have already secured the outcome. My victory is irreversible, my protection unshakable, and my deliverance undeniable.

In Jesus' name, Amen.

DAY 7

REDEEMED FROM ALL EVIL

The angel who has redeemed me from all evil, bless the lads. Let my name be named on them, and the name of my fathers Abraham and Isaac. Let them grow into a multitude upon the earth.
— Genesis 48:16 WEB

Redeeming God, Covenant-Keeping Father, I glorify Your name. You are the One who delivers from all evil, the Angel of the Lord who goes before me, who redeems my life from destruction and crowns me with loving-kindness.

Lord, I decree that evil has no inheritance in my bloodline. Every curse is reversed, every generational bondage is broken, and every evil pattern is erased. My family is redeemed and blessed in the name of Jesus.

Father, let my children and generations after me carry the mark of divine protection. Let the covenant blessings of Abraham and Isaac rest upon us. Multiply us in peace, prosperity, and holiness, and let the shadow of evil never again darken our dwelling.

Redeemer of Israel, bless my household with fruitfulness, establish us in righteousness, and enlarge our influence for Your glory. Where the enemy plotted reduction, decree increase. Where darkness spoke death, speak life abundant.

I declare that the Angel of the Lord surrounds us continually. My lineage is preserved, my destiny is redeemed, and my name is established in covenant with the living God. No evil shall prevail against us.

In Jesus' name, Amen.

WEEK 2:
ARMOR & AUTHORITY

Theme: Claiming Christ's Defense and Victory.

The believer is not left exposed to the assaults of darkness. God has furnished us with a complete armor, every piece crafted for victory. From the belt of truth to the sword of the Spirit, we are fully equipped to stand unshaken. Yet armor alone is not enough; we are also given authority—the delegated power of Christ Himself—to tread upon serpents, to silence the accuser, and to enforce heaven's decrees on earth.

This week, you will be reminded that prayer is not passive. Prayer is warfare. To put on the armor of God is to consciously step into your rightful position as a soldier of Christ. It is to refuse intimidation, to resist deception, and to boldly declare that the victory of Calvary is your inheritance. You do not fight for victory—you fight from victory.

Each day's prayer will help you fasten your armor and wield your authority. As you pray, chains will break, fiery darts will fall harmlessly, and the enemy will scatter. The power of Christ within you will silence every opposition, and you will walk as one covered by heaven's defense and empowered by divine authority.

DAY 8

CLOTHED IN DIVINE ARMOR

"Finally, be strong in the Lord, and in the strength of his
might. Put on the whole armor of God, that you may be
able to stand against the wiles of the devil... Take the
helmet of salvation, and the sword of the Spirit, which is
the word of God; with all prayer and requests, praying at
all times in the Spirit..."
— Ephesians 6:10-18 WEB

Mighty Lord of Hosts, I take my stand today clothed in Your holy armor. I will not shrink back, for You have armed me with truth, righteousness, peace, faith, salvation, and the Word of the Spirit. I declare that no weapon of darkness can pierce the covering You have given me.

I buckle around my waist the belt of truth, rejecting every lie of the enemy that seeks to twist my mind or weaken my resolve. I fasten the breastplate of righteousness, covering my heart from corruption and guarding my spirit from hidden snares. My feet are shod with the preparation of the gospel of peace; I walk in unshakable confidence that You order my steps in triumph.

I lift high the shield of faith, quenching every fiery dart of fear, disease, poverty, and confusion. I place firmly upon my head the helmet of salvation, declaring that my thoughts are sanctified and my destiny sealed by the blood of the Lamb. In my hand I wield the sword of the Spirit, cutting down every scheme of the adversary with Your eternal Word.

Lord, I pray always in the Spirit, aligning my petitions with Your will. Let the power of intercession cover my family, shielding them from ambush and hidden traps. Let every demonic assignment against my life and household be shattered by the authority of Your Spirit-filled Word.

Today, I walk in full armor. I am fortified, untouchable, and immovable. The victory of Christ surrounds me as a wall of fire. In Jesus' name, Amen.

DAY 9

AUTHORITY TO TRAMPLE

"Behold, I give you authority to tread on serpents and scorpions, and over all the power of the enemy. Nothing will in any way hurt you."
— Luke 10:19 WEB

Lion of Judah, today I rise in the authority You have entrusted to me through Christ Jesus. I declare that I tread upon every serpent and scorpion that lurks in the shadows of my life. No scheme of witchcraft, no voice of accusation, no plot of destruction shall prevail against me. You have given me power over all the works of the enemy, and I walk in it boldly.

Every serpent of generational curse is crushed under my feet. Every scorpion of sudden attack loses its sting against me. Every power of evil that rises in judgment falls broken at the sound of Your name. Lord, You have made me untouchable to the adversary, for the blood of Jesus speaks a better word over my life.

I trample down sickness, poverty, oppression, and fear. I declare that every spirit assigned to torment my family is bound and cast down. My home is sanctified ground, my body a temple of the Holy Spirit, and my destiny an altar of fire. Nothing by any means shall harm me or those who belong to me.

Father, I walk in boldness today, carrying the scepter of Your authority. Angels encamp around me; demons scatter before me;

darkness flees at the light I carry. I am a warrior who cannot be touched, for Christ has sealed my victory.

I stand fearless, for I have been authorized by heaven to conquer and to prevail. In Jesus' name, Amen.

DAY 10

HELD SECURE IN HIS HANDS

"I give eternal life to them. They will never perish, and no one will snatch them out of my hand. My Father, who has given them to me, is greater than all. No one is able to snatch them out of my Father's hand."
— John 10:28-29 WEB

Eternal Shepherd, I lift my voice with gratitude that I am held securely in Your hands. I am unshakable, unmovable, and undefeatable, for no power of darkness can snatch me away from You. You are greater than all adversaries, and Your hand is my fortress of life.

I declare that my soul will not perish. Every threat of spiritual death and destruction is silenced. Every voice of fear is rebuked. I rest under the covering of Your sovereign hand, where no enemy can reach. My destiny is sealed in You, and no evil force can rewrite my story.

My family is also safe within Your grasp. Lord, surround them with the assurance of Your eternal covenant. Let no demonic trap ensnare them, no assignment of evil break through the fortress of Your care. They are hidden in the hollow of Your mighty hand, preserved from ruin and despair.

Every chain of fear and intimidation is broken. I walk in the confidence of eternal life and victory. I stand in the assurance that the Father's grip will never release me to the enemy's plans.

O Lord, my Defender and Keeper, I proclaim this day that I am untouchable, guarded by Your hand, and established in everlasting triumph. In Jesus' name, Amen.

DAY 11

OVERCOME BY THE BLOOD

"They overcame him because of the Lamb's blood, and because of the word of their testimony. They didn't love their life, even to death."
— Revelation 12:11 WEB

Mighty Redeemer, I lift high the banner of the blood of Jesus. I declare today that by the blood of the Lamb, I overcome every evil power, every satanic accusation, every chain of bondage, and every curse spoken against my life. The blood speaks victory, the blood speaks life, and the blood speaks power on my behalf.

By the blood, I silence the accuser. Every voice that rises against me is condemned. Every demonic decree is annulled. I testify that I belong to Christ, and His blood is my eternal covering. I overcome by the testimony of His finished work on the cross.

Lord, I release the blood of Jesus over my family, my children, my home, and my destiny. The blood breaks the grip of generational curses. The blood dismantles assignments of sickness, oppression, and calamity. The blood declares that we are untouchable, protected, and sanctified.

I renounce fear of death, fear of failure, and fear of the future. My allegiance is to Christ alone. My life is poured out for His glory, and no evil shall shorten my days. I embrace the victory of the blood that never loses its power.

Today, I decree that the adversary is defeated, my testimony is unstoppable, and the blood of Jesus forever secures my triumph. In Jesus' name, Amen.

DAY 12

SUBMIT AND RESIST

"Be subject therefore to God. Resist the devil, and he will
flee from you."
— James 4:7 WEB

Almighty God, I bow in surrender before Your throne of grace. I
yield my will, my desires, my thoughts, and my actions completely
to You. I submit every part of my life to Your Lordship, declaring
that I am consecrated for Your glory.

With holy boldness, I resist the devil. I renounce every temptation,
break every chain of compromise, and silence every whisper of
darkness. I decree that the adversary has no foothold in my life, my
marriage, my family, or my destiny. His schemes are scattered, his
lies are exposed, and his power is broken.

Lord, I submit my household to Your covering. Every hidden
agenda of the enemy is uncovered and destroyed. Every plot to sow
division, corruption, or despair is overturned by Your mighty hand.
My family walks in purity, holiness, and victory, for we belong to
You.

As I resist the forces of darkness, let the fire of the Holy Spirit blaze
within me. Strengthen my spirit to stand firm, my heart to stay
pure, and my voice to proclaim truth without fear. Let the devil flee
in terror at the sight of Your Spirit's authority in my life.

I am a submitted warrior, a yielded vessel, and an unshakable child of God. The devil has no place here, for my God reigns. In Jesus' name, Amen.

DAY 13

KEPT FROM THE EVIL ONE

"We know that whoever is born of God doesn't sin, but he who was born of God keeps himself, and the evil one doesn't touch him."
— 1 John 5:18 WEB

Holy Father, I declare that I am born of You, redeemed by the blood of Christ, and sanctified by the Spirit of grace. Because I am born of God, I am untouchable to the powers of darkness. The evil one cannot lay hold of me, for I am preserved by the hand of the Righteous One.

I decree that sin will not rule over me. Every chain of iniquity is shattered, every cycle of compromise broken, and every snare of temptation burned away. I walk in purity, covered by the holiness of Christ, and my life reflects the glory of the Father.

Lord, I cover my household with this promise. The evil one cannot touch my children, my spouse, my loved ones, or my possessions. We are sealed in covenant blood, preserved in righteousness, and established in divine protection.

Let the fire of Your holiness keep me vigilant and pure. Let the shield of Your grace guard me from every arrow of corruption. I proclaim that I am a child of God who walks in victory, righteousness, and consecration.

O Keeper of my soul, I rejoice that I am beyond the reach of Satan's grip. I am hidden in You, secured in Christ, and empowered by the Spirit. The evil one cannot touch me. In Jesus' name, Amen.

DAY 14

More Than a Conqueror

"No, in all these things, we are more than conquerors
through him who loved us."
— Romans 8:37 WEB

Glorious King, I rise with a shout of triumph that in every battle, in
every trial, and in every affliction, I am more than a conqueror
through Christ who loves me. I do not merely survive; I reign in
victory. I do not just endure; I overcome with authority and power.

Lord, I proclaim that no attack of the enemy can reduce me to
defeat. Every scheme collapses, every snare breaks, and every curse
dissolves before the strength of Your love. Because You love me, I
am untouchable, victorious, and unstoppable.

I declare that my family is covered in this triumph. Where the
enemy plots ruin, You bring restoration. Where he designs
destruction, You bring deliverance. Where he sows despair, You
release overwhelming joy. We are conquerors together, standing
unbroken and unshaken.

Father, I rise above sickness, poverty, oppression, and fear. I walk in
the reality that Christ's love empowers me to trample down
strongholds and claim spoils of victory. I am more than a
conqueror, established as a warrior of light in a world of darkness.

O God of victory, I embrace this identity with joy and boldness. I
will never bow to defeat, for love has lifted me higher than every
scheme of evil. In Jesus' name, Amen.

WEEK 3:
RESIST & STAND PURE

Theme: Guarding Heart, Mind, and Conduct.

Evil does not only come through external attacks; it often seeks entry through the subtle temptations of the heart and mind. The enemy longs to plant seeds of compromise, impurity, fear, or pride. Yet God has called you to resist, to stand firm, and to walk undefiled in a world drenched in sin. Purity is not weakness—it is strength. Holiness is not bondage—it is freedom.

This week focuses on fortifying your inner life. To resist the devil is to actively guard your heart with diligence, to renew your mind with God's Word, and to let the fire of the Spirit keep you consecrated. Through prayer, you will cleanse the gateways of your life—your thoughts, your speech, your actions—and dedicate them fully to God.

Every prayer this week is both a wall and a weapon. You will declare that temptation will not master you, that hidden snares will not trap you, and that your steps will not slip. You will claim the purity that empowers authority, the holiness that keeps you untouchable, and the grace that enables you to walk blameless in this generation.

DAY 15

WAY OF ESCAPE

"No temptation has taken you except what is common to man. God is faithful, who will not allow you to be tempted above what you are able, but will with the temptation also make the way of escape, that you may be able to endure it."
— 1 Corinthians 10:13 WEB

Faithful Father, my Rock and Deliverer, I lift my voice in holy confidence. You are the unshakable refuge who never abandons Your children to the snares of the enemy. Today I declare that I will not be crushed under the weight of trial, nor will my household be swallowed by the deceit of sin. For You have set boundaries around temptation, and the adversary cannot cross the lines You have drawn.

Lord, I receive Your way of escape in every hidden snare the enemy lays before me. Let my eyes be opened to discern his traps before I stumble. May my spirit rise strong, empowered by Your Spirit, to reject every invitation of darkness. Father, I claim victory in the same power that raised Jesus from the dead—power that breaks chains and severs cords of compromise.

By Your covenant mercy, I declare that no addiction, no secret struggle, no generational curse will overpower me or my family. The blood of Jesus speaks a better word over us, and it silences every accusation of hell. In the heat of battle, when fiery darts come suddenly, I will not faint, for Your strength girds me.

I prophesy that I am walking out of every pit. My house will not be consumed by hidden bondage but will stand pure, holy, and untouchable. Temptation may come, but it will not conquer us. Sin may knock, but it will not reign. My family and I are marked by the covenant blood, destined to endure and overcome.

In Jesus' name, Amen.

DAY 16

NO LASTING HARM

"No mischief shall happen to the righteous, but the wicked shall be filled with evil."
— Proverbs 12:21 WEB

Righteous Judge of all the earth, I rise in the confidence of Your word that declares no evil shall befall the righteous. I stand clothed in the righteousness of Christ, and I decree that my life and my family are shielded from calamity. We will not be victims of evil plots, nor shall we be casualties of hidden mischief.

Lord, I pull down every evil assignment fashioned against us. Let the snares of the wicked return upon their own heads. Let the pits they dig swallow their schemes. For my portion is not disaster but divine preservation. The curse of destruction will not light upon my dwelling; instead, the blessing of protection surrounds us like a wall of fire.

I decree that the covering of Christ renders my home untouchable. Sickness will not take root, tragedy will not lodge, and misfortune will not abide in our gates. The Spirit of the Lord raises a standard against every weapon forged in secret councils. Their conspiracies dissolve under the power of Your name.

Father, I declare that wickedness shall never dominate my household. While they are filled with evil, we are filled with peace, joy, and righteousness. I stand in prophetic assurance that my family shall see the downfall of every adversary. Their attempts will crumble, and their boasting will be silenced.

Today I lift my shield of faith and declare: we are divinely guarded, divinely exempted, and divinely secured. Evil shall not prosper against us. Mischief shall not draw near us. We walk in holy immunity by the power of Christ's righteousness.

In Jesus' name, Amen.

DAY 17

ANGELIC ENCIRCLEMENT

"The angel of Yahweh encamps around those who fear him, and delivers them."
— Psalm 34:7 WEB

Lord of Hosts, Commander of the armies of heaven, I exalt Your mighty power. You have appointed angelic guardians around those who fear You, and I declare that my family and I are encircled in heavenly defense. No weapon formed against us can penetrate the wall of fire You have set.

Father, I summon Your angelic hosts to encamp round about my home, to stand guard at every entryway, and to patrol the unseen realms where darkness prowls. Let the swords of fire drawn by Your messengers cut down every spiritual pursuer, and let their presence scatter the schemes of darkness.

I declare divine deliverance over my bloodline. Whatever snares have been set in the night, whatever curses whispered in secrecy, the angels of the Lord overturn them by their charge. Let the unseen hand of heaven break the chains of affliction and uproot every wicked planting.

Even when terror prowls in shadows, we shall not fear, for the Lord encamps with us. His armies are stationed in our defense. Father, I decree that evil cannot breach the covenant hedge around my life. My children are secured, my household preserved, and my destiny shielded by angelic presence.

I prophesy today that no ambush will succeed, no assault will penetrate, no siege will prevail. The angels of Yahweh war on our behalf, and their encampment ensures our victory. We are delivered, shielded, and untouchable in Christ.

In Jesus' name, Amen.

DAY 18

RESCUED FROM TRIALS

"The Lord knows how to deliver the godly out of temptation and to keep the unrighteous under punishment to the day of judgment."
— 2 Peter 2:9 WEB

All-Knowing God, You see every snare before it forms. You know every scheme of the wicked before it arises, and You have ordained deliverance for the godly. Today, I rest in Your covenant knowledge and power. My life and my family are not abandoned to the assaults of evil but are divinely rescued.

Father, I decree that the plans of darkness are frustrated. Every attempt to trap my mind, pollute my purity, or ensnare my children is broken. The wicked may gather, but You keep them under judgment, unable to execute their schemes. You are the Deliverer who rescues Your own with a mighty hand.

I declare over my household that no temptation will overpower us. By Your Spirit, we are strengthened to reject the crooked path. By Your wisdom, we discern the lies of the adversary. You draw us out of every net and guide us into paths of holiness.

Lord, let the fire of Your holiness burn away the residue of every past bondage. Let the blood of Jesus silence accusations and shield us from hidden arrows. You are faithful to preserve us when the enemy plots, and You will not allow his designs to prevail.

I prophesy that my family and I will walk in purity, untouchable by corruption. We will endure by the strength of Your Spirit, and every plan of the wicked will backfire upon them. We are the redeemed, delivered, and preserved for Your glory.

In Jesus' name, Amen.

DAY 19

FAITHFUL GUARD

"But the Lord is faithful, who will establish you and guard
you from the evil one."
— 2 Thessalonians 3:3 WEB

Faithful Lord, Covenant Keeper, I stand in awe of Your unfailing
protection. You are the unchanging One who surrounds me with
steadfast love. Today, I lift my banner in prophetic decree: my
family and I are established, strengthened, and guarded from every
assault of the evil one.

I call forth Your divine stability in every area of my life. Where the
enemy seeks to shake my foundations, You establish me on Christ
the Solid Rock. Where darkness seeks to uproot my faith, You
anchor me deep in Your Word. No storm, no demon, no whisper of
the accuser can unsettle me.

Father, I receive Your guarding presence. Let the evil one find no
access point in my heart, no foothold in my mind, no entrance in
my home. Build a wall of fire around my family and let Your glory
be our defense. Keep us from deception, seduction, and distraction.

I declare that no enchantment or divination shall prosper against
us. Satan's arrows shall fall powerless, and his snares shall wither.
You are faithful to preserve us in every battle, faithful to silence the
roar of the adversary.

I prophesy that the enemy will flee in seven directions. My
household is marked as untouchable, my children are secured, and

our destiny is sealed in Christ. Faithful Lord, You guard our coming in and our going out, shielding us from all evil.

In Jesus' name, Amen.

DAY 20

THE LORD DELIVERS

"And the Lord will deliver me from every evil work, and will preserve me for his heavenly Kingdom; to whom be the glory forever and ever. Amen."
— 2 Timothy 4:18 WEB

Deliverer of Zion, I glorify Your holy name. You are the One who rescues from every evil work, who preserves Your children until we step into glory. Today, I rise as a warrior clothed in Your promise, declaring that I and my household are preserved by Your power.

Lord, I declare that no evil work—whether plotted in darkness, spoken in malice, or executed in hatred—will prosper against me. You deliver me from snares seen and unseen. You cut off the cords of wickedness and silence every storm of destruction aimed at my life.

Preserve me, O Lord, in my journey. Keep my household steadfast, covered under the shadow of Your wings. Let Your heavenly Kingdom agenda manifest in us, and let no demonic hand derail our assignment. I declare that preservation is my portion, and every plan of the enemy collapses under Your might.

Father, I renounce every work of darkness contending against my family. Let it be swallowed by the power of Your Spirit. Let every curse be overturned by the blood of Jesus. We are preserved for Your glory, and the schemes of hell cannot rewrite our destiny.

I prophesy longevity, divine covering, and unstoppable progress. The enemy's arrows will miss their mark, but we will march forward, delivered and preserved, until we stand triumphant in Your Kingdom.

In Jesus' name, Amen.

DAY 21

STANDING AGAINST THE ROAR

"Be sober and self-controlled. Be watchful. Your adversary
the devil walks around like a roaring lion, seeking whom
he may devour. Withstand him steadfast in your faith,
knowing that your brothers who are in the world are
undergoing the same sufferings."
— 1 Peter 5:8-9 WEB

Mighty God, Captain of my salvation, I rise in vigilance. I will not
be lulled into slumber, for I know the adversary prowls like a
roaring lion. Yet, his roar shall not consume me, for the Lion of
Judah roars stronger on my behalf.

Father, I declare sobriety over my spirit and alertness over my mind.
I will not yield to distraction or deception. I bind the devourer and
resist him steadfast in the faith. His roar may sound, but it is hollow
before the voice of the Lord. His threats may come, but they
crumble under the weight of Christ's victory.

I stand in solidarity with the saints of God across the earth. We are
not alone in the battle; we are an army marching together under the
banner of Christ. Together we resist the devil, and together we
prevail.

Lord, fortify my faith until it is unshakable. Let my prayers thunder
against the gates of hell. Let my testimony silence the accuser. I
declare that the adversary will find no opening in my life. His plans

to devour my household shall backfire, and his threats will be silenced.

I prophesy holy boldness in my walk. The roar of fear is broken, the snare of intimidation shattered, and the devourer cast down. My family and I will not be prey but victors in Christ, standing steadfast until the day of triumph.

In Jesus' name, Amen.

DAY 22

Kept in the World

"I pray not that you would take them from the world, but
that you would keep them from the evil one."
— John 17:15 WEB

Holy Father, Keeper of my soul, I lift the words of Jesus, my
Intercessor, who prayed for our preservation. I stand in this
covenant promise that though I remain in the world, I am not
abandoned to its corruption. You keep me and my family from the
grasp of the evil one.

Lord, I declare separation from the spirit of the age. Though
darkness increases, it cannot overtake us. Though wickedness
multiplies, it cannot consume us. I am covered by the prayer of
Christ Himself, the One whose intercession never fails.

Father, shield my household from defilement. Guard our minds
from deception, our hearts from compromise, and our steps from
the crooked path. Let the evil one find no entry into our gates. Place
Your seal upon our lives and let the blood of Jesus mark us as
untouchable.

I decree that though the world rages, I and my family are hidden in
the secret place. While others stumble in corruption, we are upheld
in righteousness. While many fall to temptation, we are preserved
in purity.

I prophesy that no scheme of hell, no snare of deception, no weapon
of the evil one will succeed against us. The prayer of Jesus ensures

our victory, and His word secures our destiny. We are kept, preserved, and covered until the day of His return.

In Jesus' name, Amen.

WEEK 4:
PROMISES & WARFARE DECLARATIONS

Theme: God's Pledges and Offensive Truth.

God's Word is more than comfort—it is a weapon. His promises are not mere suggestions; they are unshakable decrees sealed by the blood of Jesus. Every "It is written" is a sword in the Spirit's hand, a weapon that cuts down lies, demolishes strongholds, and enforces heaven's rule over the earth. This week, you will learn to take those promises from the pages of Scripture and turn them into declarations of victory over every battle you face.

Prayer becomes powerful when it is rooted in God's unchanging pledges. Here, you will not merely ask—you will decree. You will not beg—you will enforce. You will rise to your rightful place as one who speaks with the authority of heaven, reminding the enemy that his defeat is final, his lies are broken, and his power is nullified.

As you press into these prayers, expect breakthroughs. Expect doors of deliverance to open. Expect chains to fall and captives to be released. For when the Word of God is declared in faith, angels move, demons tremble, and heaven responds. This final week will position you to walk out of this 30-day journey with confidence, knowing that you are not only shielded from evil but also empowered to destroy its works.

DAY 23

GUARD MY LIFE

Jabez called on the God of Israel, saying, "Oh that you would bless me indeed, and enlarge my border! Let your hand be with me, and keep me from evil, that I may not cause pain!" God granted him that which he requested.
—1 Chronicles 4:10 WEB

Almighty Father, the God of Israel, the Keeper of my soul, I rise with boldness to declare that I am not a victim of evil but a vessel chosen for blessing. I decree that Your hand rests mightily upon me, steering me away from snares and plots of darkness. I will not walk into traps laid by the enemy, for Your covenant shields me.

By the authority of Christ's finished work, I command every evil arrow shot against my destiny and my family to backfire. I release fire upon every wicked scheme that seeks to cut short my life or reduce my influence. Evil will not prevail in my borders. My household is fenced in by the wall of Your divine fire.

Lord, enlarge the territory of my influence and cause every expansion to be free from sorrow. Where pain has tried to enter, I declare healing and peace. Where curses once reigned, I enforce blessing. Every generational affliction seeking to follow me into my enlargement breaks now under the blood of Jesus.

I prophesy divine expansion over my family, ministry, and work. Evil hands will not shrink my harvest. Powers of darkness will not sabotage my joy. I receive blessed increase that carries no grief.

O God of Jabez, grant me this request: let evil find no place in me or around me. Establish me as untouchable, a testimony of divine preservation.

In Jesus' name, Amen.

DAY 24

DELIVER ME FROM THE EVIL ONE

Bring us not into temptation, but deliver us from the evil one. For yours is the Kingdom, the power, and the glory forever. Amen.
—Matthew 6:13 WEB

Eternal King, Ruler of Heaven and Earth, I lift my cry to You, the Deliverer of my soul. You are the One who breaks the grip of evil and silences the power of the wicked. Today I declare that temptation shall not master me, and the evil one shall not rule over my household.

By the authority of Christ, I sever every chain of seduction, compromise, and deception. I cancel every contract of darkness aimed at corrupting my destiny. I declare that the snares of the evil one are shattered. Temptations designed to bring me low are stripped of power. The way of escape that You have provided is opened before me, and I walk in it triumphantly.

I stand in intercession for my family. Lord, deliver them from the hands of the wicked. Evil will not swallow their glory, and temptation will not abort their destinies. I cover every member of my bloodline in the blood of Jesus, declaring them untouchable to demonic lures and satanic traps.

Father, I enthrone You in my life. Yours is the Kingdom—Your authority rules me. Yours is the power—Your might defends me.

Yours is the glory—Your light shines on me. In Your presence, the evil one flees seven ways.

I decree today that no demon will write the last chapter of my story. My testimony shall be victory, purity, and dominion through Christ.

In Jesus' name, Amen.

DAY 25

PEACE FROM ALL ADVERSARIES

"You know that David my father could not build a house
for Yahweh his God because of the wars which were
around him on every side, until Yahweh put his enemies
under the soles of his feet. But now Yahweh my God has
given me rest on every side. There is no adversary, and no
evil occurrence."
—1 Kings 5:3-4 WEB

Lord of Hosts, God of peace, I lift my voice in thanksgiving for the
rest You have ordained for me. I decree that the days of endless
warfare in my family line are over. The battles that consumed my
fathers shall not consume me. By Your mighty hand, You bring my
adversaries under my feet, and You silence every evil occurrence.

Father, I speak to the atmosphere of my life: let divine rest break
forth. Let the sword of wickedness be broken. I command every
storm stirred by the enemy against my destiny to cease. My home
shall not be a battleground of strife, sickness, or affliction. The
adversaries that rose in the night to swallow my joy shall be
swallowed by the fire of God.

I proclaim that my season is shifting into rest. The time of war is
replaced with the time of building. Like Solomon, I will build with
clean hands, free from distractions of evil warfare. My children will
not inherit my battles, but they will inherit the peace of the Lord.

Every evil occurrence programmed into my future is erased. Accidents, disasters, calamities, sudden death, and hidden traps are overturned by the blood of Jesus. I walk in the divine canopy of rest on every side.

Lord, establish me in peace, and let my life be a testimony that You fight for Your children until every adversary bows.

In Jesus' name, Amen.

DAY 26

FORTIFIED AGAINST THE WICKED

> I will make you to this people a fortified bronze wall. They will fight against you, but they will not prevail against you; for I am with you to save you and to deliver you," says Yahweh. "I will deliver you out of the hand of the wicked, and I will redeem you out of the hand of the terrible."
> —Jeremiah 15:20-21 WEB

Mighty Deliverer, Fortress of my soul, I decree today that I am a fortified bronze wall against every adversary. Though battles may rise, none shall prevail. You are with me to save, and Your word is my impregnable defense.

I nullify the hand of the wicked stretched against my life. Every evil altar raised to war against me is torn down by holy fire. Terrible powers seeking to intimidate my destiny are bound and cast down. I am not a prey, but a warrior equipped with divine backing.

Over my family, I declare supernatural deliverance. The wicked will not have the last word. Invisible chains binding their progress are broken. Hidden snares designed to keep them captive are destroyed. I prophesy liberty and redemption in every area where darkness tried to enslave us.

Lord, You are my Redeemer. You ransom me from the grip of the terrible. I am covered in the blood of Jesus, marked as untouchable. Let my enemies see and tremble, for You dwell with me. Their plots shall scatter, and their weapons shall rust.

Today I rise as Your fortified servant, unyielding in the face of opposition, because You fight for me. My victory is established, and my redemption is secure.

In Jesus' name, Amen.

DAY 27

SNATCHED FROM THE SNARE

Blessed be Yahweh, who has not given us as a prey to their teeth. Our soul has escaped like a bird out of the fowler's snare. The snare is broken, and we have escaped.
—Psalms 124:6-7 WEB

Glorious Deliverer, I lift my praise to You who has not abandoned me to the jaws of the wicked. I am not their prey, nor will my household be food for their destruction. You break the fowler's snare and grant us escape.

Father, I decree that every trap set against me is shattered. The teeth of the devourer are broken, and his appetite for my soul is frustrated. Like a bird set free, I soar into liberty. I declare that the net of affliction, poverty, sickness, and death is torn asunder. No cage of darkness shall contain my destiny.

Over my children, I speak escape. Over my spouse and family, I proclaim liberty. Evil monitoring spirits lose their grip. Wicked contracts over my lineage are annulled. The snare is broken—forever.

Lord, I rise in prophetic boldness to declare that every ambush planned against me in secret is exposed and overturned. The paths laid with traps become highways of testimony. Instead of capture, I experience promotion. Instead of loss, I reap restoration.

Blessed be Your name, O Lord. You have lifted my head above the hunter's snare. You have made me untouchable to the powers that lurk in the shadows. I walk in freedom, victory, and praise.

In Jesus' name, Amen.

DAY 28

NO WEAPON SHALL STAND

No weapon that is formed against you will prevail; and you will condemn every tongue that rises against you in judgment. This is the heritage of Yahweh's servants, and their righteousness is of me," says Yahweh.
—Isaiah 54:17 WEB

Almighty Defender, I decree this day that no weapon forged in darkness shall prosper against me. Every spiritual artillery, every satanic device, every evil invention aimed at my destruction is rendered powerless. By the authority of Your Word, I disarm them now.

I rise to condemn every tongue of accusation and judgment. Evil decrees spoken against my family, curses whispered in the dark, and judgments written in secret are reversed. I silence them with the authority of Christ's blood. No verdict of hell shall stand over my life.

Lord, I claim my heritage as Your servant: protection, righteousness, and victory. This inheritance cannot be stolen. My children walk in it, my household thrives in it, and my destiny flourishes in it. The shield of righteousness covers me, making me untouchable to the arrows of the night.

Every satanic alliance formed against me scatters. Weapons buried, weapons projected, and weapons invoked—all collapse in futility. The enemy shall watch in frustration as their devices backfire.

Father, I decree that my life will display the heritage of the redeemed: victory without defeat, progress without hindrance, and peace without interruption.

In Jesus' name, Amen.

DAY 29

Fear Not, For I Am With You

Don't you be afraid, for I am with you. Don't be dismayed,
for I am your God. I will strengthen you. Yes, I will help
you. Yes, I will uphold you with the right hand of my
righteousness.

—Isaiah 41:10 WEB

Father of Strength, I bow before You as my Helper, my Upholder,
and my Strengthener. I decree today that fear has no place in my
life. I am not dismayed, for You, O God, are with me.

I release the fire of God against every spirit of fear sent to paralyze
my progress. I break the grip of intimidation and terror. The evil
one shall not manipulate my emotions. Anxiety, panic, and torment
dissolve in the presence of Your Word.

Lord, I draw upon Your strength. Where I am weak, You infuse me
with divine might. Where my family is weary, You uphold us with
Your right hand of righteousness. I prophesy divine boldness over
my children, that they shall not cower before evil but rise in courage
and holiness.

Father, let every weapon of fear boomerang on its sender. Let the
very intimidation of the enemy become his own destruction. I
declare my mind fortified, my spirit strengthened, and my heart
anchored in peace.

You, O Lord, are my righteousness, my fortress, and my support. I will not fall, for You uphold me. I will not faint, for You empower me. Fear has been banished, and faith has arisen.

In Jesus' name, Amen.

DAY 30

Pulling Down Strongholds

For though we walk in the flesh, we don't wage war according to the flesh; for the weapons of our warfare are not of the flesh, but mighty before God to the throwing down of strongholds, throwing down imaginations and every high thing that is exalted against the knowledge of God, and bringing every thought into captivity to the obedience of Christ.

—2 Corinthians 10:3-5 WEB

Mighty Man of War, I rise with the weapons of Your Spirit, declaring that my battle is not carnal but spiritual. I decree the pulling down of strongholds that have long resisted my progress. Every fortress of evil is shattered under the weight of Your power.

I demolish imaginations and lies that exalt themselves against the knowledge of Christ in my life. I refuse every satanic suggestion, every deceptive voice, every thought designed to corrupt my purity. I bring every thought captive to the obedience of Christ.

Lord, I lift my voice as a warrior. I confront demonic systems resisting my family. I command ancestral strongholds of idolatry, poverty, infirmity, and confusion to crumble. Generational lies are torn down. Evil patterns are broken.

By the blood of Jesus, I release a prophetic decree: my household is liberated. Minds are renewed, and hearts are surrendered to Christ. Every high place erected against God in my lineage is dismantled.

I take up the mighty weapons of faith, the Word, and the Spirit. I wage victorious warfare. My victory is not partial but complete, for Christ reigns in me.

In Jesus' name, Amen.

EPILOGUE

The completion of this 30-day journey is not the end—it is the beginning of a lifestyle of vigilance, empowerment, and divine protection. You have learned to pray with focus, to speak Scripture prophetically, and to declare God's authority over every scheme of the enemy. These prayers have been designed to equip you to stand firm long after the last page is turned.

Carry this practice forward daily. Let the principles of shelter, armor, purity, and declarations become habits, not just exercises. Keep the Word active in your life, and let your voice continue to enforce heaven's decrees over every part of your existence. Every step you take in faith builds a spiritual environment where evil cannot gain ground.

Remember, the One who has kept you thus far will continue to keep you. His hand is your covering, His Word your weapon, and His Spirit your guide. Stand boldly, pray consistently, and live untouchable. The life of victory you have begun in these pages is already yours.

In Jesus' name, Amen.

.

ENCOURAGE OTHERS WITH YOUR STORY

If this prayer guide has strengthened your faith, deepened your intercession, or helped you stand in the gap, would you consider leaving a short review on Amazon? Your feedback not only encourages others but also helps more believers discover this resource and join in the prayer movement. Every review—just a few sentences—makes a difference. Thank you for being part of this movement.

MORE FROM PRAYERSCRIPTS

COMMAND YOUR DESTINY SERIES

Command Your Morning:

30 Days of Prayers and Declarations to Seize Your Day and Shape Your Destiny

There is a battle over every morning—and every believer must choose to either drift into the day or command it.

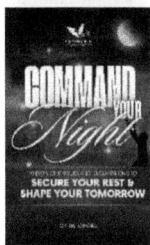

Command Your Night:

30 Days of Prayers and Declarations to Secure Your Rest and Shape Your Tomorrow

Every night is a spiritual battlefield—what you do before you sleep can determine the course of your tomorrow.

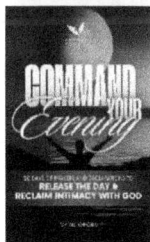

Command Your Evening:

30 Days of Prayers and Declarations to Release the Day and Reclaim Intimacy with God

There is a battle over every transition—and evening is one of the most spiritually neglected.

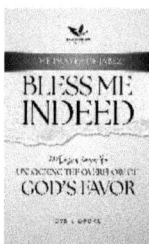

Bless Me Indeed:

Unlocking the Overflow of God's Favor

What if you could activate God's favor in your life today and walk in blessings that surpass your wildest expectations?

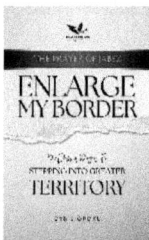

Enlarge My Border:

Stepping Into Greater Territory

Do you feel like you're living beneath your full potential? Do limitations, setbacks, and invisible barriers keep you from stepping into all God has promised? It's time to lift your cry for enlargement.

May Your Hand Be With Me:

Living Under Divine Power and Presence

What happens when the mighty hand of God rests upon your life? Doors open that no man can shut. Strength rises where weakness once prevailed. Guidance comes in the midst of confusion, and protection surrounds you in every battle.

Keep Me From Evil:

Standing Untouchable in Spiritual Warfare

What if the enemy's plans could never touch you or your family? Imagine walking through life completely protected, untouchable, and victorious—no matter what schemes are formed against you.

No More Pain:

Breaking Free from Suffering into Wholeness

Have you been carrying the weight of sorrow, disappointment, or hidden wounds for far too long? Do cycles of pain seem to repeat in your life, your marriage, or your family?

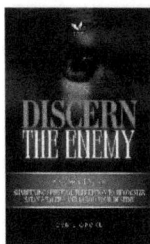

Discern the Enemy:

Sharpening Spiritual Perception to Recognize Satan's Tactics and Guard Your Destiny

The greatest danger is not the enemy you can see—it is the one you cannot. Can you recognize the enemy before he strikes?

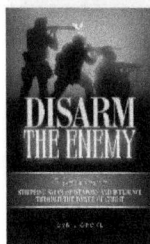

Disarm the Enemy:

Stripping Satan of Weapons and Influence Through the Power of Christ

Are you tired of feeling like the enemy has the upper hand in your life? It's time to take back your ground, silence the lies of darkness, and walk in the unstoppable authority of Christ.

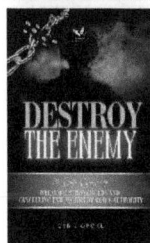

Destroy the Enemy:

Breaking Strongholds and Cancelling Evil Works by God's Authority

Are you tired of living under the weight of unseen battles? It's time to rise up and destroy the enemy's works in your life.

Deliver from the Enemy:

Calling on God's Power for Freedom, Rescue, and Lasting Victory

Break free from spiritual attacks and experience God's mighty deliverance in every battle.

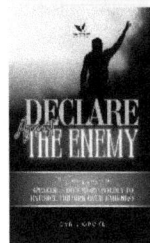

Declare Against the Enemy:

Speaking God's Word Boldly to Enforce Triumph Over Darkness

What if you could silence the enemy's schemes, protect your family, and walk boldly into every God-ordained assignment with unshakable authority?

Scriptures & Prayers for Deliverance from Trouble:

40 Days of Prayer for When Life Feels Overwhelming

Are you walking through a season where life feels heavy and your prayers feel weak?

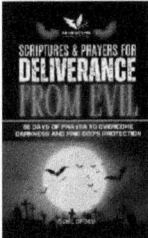

Scriptures & Prayers for Deliverance from Evil:

50 Days of Prayer to Overcome Darkness and Find God's Protection

When darkness presses in, how do you pray?

Scriptures & Prayers for Engaging the Enemy:

70 Days of Prayer to Rebuke the Enemy and Release God's Power

You weren't called to run from the battle—you were anointed to win it.

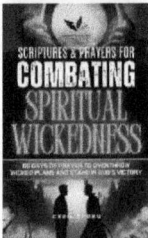

Scriptures & Prayers for Combating Spiritual Wickedness:

50 Days of Prayer to Overthrow Wicked Plans and Stand in God's Victory

Are you facing opposition that feels deeper than the natural? You're not imagining it—and you're not powerless.

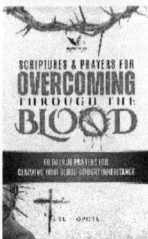

Scriptures & Prayers for Overcoming Through the Blood:

60 Days of Prayers for Claiming Your Blood-Bought Inheritance

You were never meant to fight sin, fear, or Satan in your own strength.

Standing in the Gap for Covenant Awakening:

30 Days of Prayer for National Repentance, Righteous Leadership & God's Sovereign Rule

What if your prayers could help turn the tide of a nation?

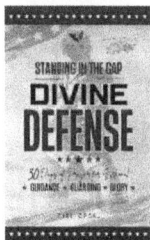

Standing in the Gap for Divine Defense:

30 Days of Prayer for National Guidance, Guarding & Glory

When the foundations of a nation feel as if they're shaking, prayer is the strongest fortress you can build.

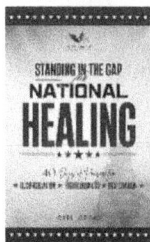

Standing in the Gap for National Healing:

40 Days of Prayer for Reconciliation, Righteousness, and Restoration

What if your prayers could help heal a nation? What if God is waiting for someone—like you—to stand in the gap?

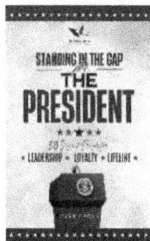

Standing in the Gap for The President:

50 Days of Prayer for Leadership, Loyalty, and Lifeline

When a nation's leader is under spiritual siege, will you answer the call to stand in the gap?

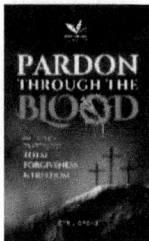

Pardon Through the Blood:

60 Days of Prayers for Total Forgiveness and Freedom

Guilt is a prison. The blood of Jesus holds the key.

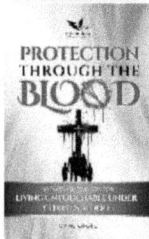

Protection Through the Blood:

60 Days of Prayers for Living Untouchable Under Christ's Blood

You are not helpless. You are not exposed. You are covered—completely—by the blood of Jesus.

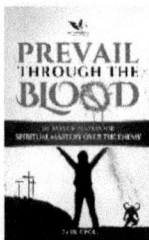

Prevail Through the Blood:

60 Days of Prayers for Spiritual Mastery Over the Enemy

What if every scheme of the enemy against your life could be dismantled—by one unstoppable weapon?

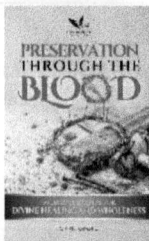

Preservation Through the Blood:

60 Days of Prayers for Divine Healing and Wholeness

Unlock Lasting Healing and Wholeness Through the Blood of Jesus

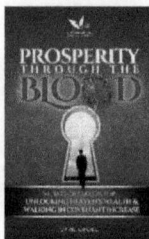

Prosperity Through the Blood:

60 Days of Prayers for Unlocking Heaven's Wealth and Walking in Covenant Increase

You were redeemed for more than survival—you were redeemed to prosper.

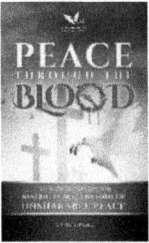

Peace Through the Blood:

60 Days of Prayers for Resting in the Covenant of Unshakable Peace

Are you ready to silence every storm of the mind, heart, and home—once and for all?